This Notebook Belongs To:

_____   _____

THE OLD FARMER'S ALMANAC

GARDENING

NOTEBOOK

Chronicle Your Garden Day by Day

Dedication

to John B. Pierce, Jr.,
Devoted Gardener and Publisher.

Published by Sellers Publishing, Inc.

161 John Roberts Road, South Portland, ME 04106
Visit us at www.sellerspublishing.com • E-mail: rsp@rsvp.com

© 2017 Sellers Publishing, Inc.
Text © Yankee Publishing Incorporated
Color Illustrations © 2017 Kristin Kest
Managing Editor: Mary L. Baldwin
Production: Charlotte Cromwell
All rights reserved.

ISBN-13: 978-1-4162-4611-4

Printed and bound in China.

10 9 8 7 6 5 4 3 2 1

THE OLD FARMER'S ALMANAC

GARDENING

NOTEBOOK

Chronicle Your Garden Day by Day

PLUS FACTS, TIPS & GARDEN LORE

SELLERS
PUBLISHING

January 1

_F_irst-of-the-year bulbs peeking up through the snow are welcome signs that spring is coming. Snowdrops, crocuses, and winter aconites look splendid when planted en masse under a tree, along a border, or down a slope, or when tucked into crevasses in a rock garden. They do well in containers, too! Choose a site in full sun or partial shade. Plant the bulbs in fall for a late winter or early spring display.

January 2

_B_romeliads, such as the pineapple, are primarily tropical plants. Most species flower only once, at which point they stop producing leaves. Small plantlets, called "pups," then develop, usually at the base of the leaves, and eventually form roots. When they reach one-third to one-half the size of the mother plant, they can be removed, as close to the mom as possible, with a sharp knife and then transplanted. The mother plant may survive for one or two generations.

January 3

*I*f your overwintering geraniums are becoming spindly, cut them back by half and move them to a cool spot with brighter light.

January 4

Notes

Sow seeds of pansy, verbena, carnation, salvia, and impatiens indoors now for early spring bloom.

January 5

*T*he female plants of *Ilex verticillata,* the winterberry holly, show bright-red berries on bare branches from late fall through January.

January 6

Notes

Walk the boundaries of your property and check for winter damage. Remove broken branches and reinforce shrub protection.

January 7

Black-oil sunflower seeds are the best-loved of all bird feed. They have a higher meat-to-shell ratio and fat content than the striped types, and birds can crack them open more easily.

January 8

To Be a Bee

Q: How many honeybees normally live in a colony?

A: That depends on the season. In winter, there might be from 5,000 to 10,000 bees living in a colony. In early summer, there could be 60,000 or more. The population also depends on the health of the colony, age of the queen, availability of resources, and temperature.

January 9

*T*ime to organize seed-starting supplies for the upcoming season.

January 10

NOTES

*S*ay It With Flowers.
January's flower, the snowdrop, means consolation
in the language of flowers.

January 11

*D*eep snow in winter, tall grain in summer.

January 12

NOTES

*J*unipers bear berrylike cones. They grow well in poor soil and are unaffected by average winters.

January 13

Traditionally, this is the coldest day of the year.

January 14

Moonflowers are tender vines with large, fragrant, white flowers that open at night.

January 15

_T_ he 'Wolf Eyes' cultivar of Chinese dogwood (*Cornus kousa*) has white, star-shape flowers, red-orange fruit, and variegated leaves that turn pink to red in autumn.

January 16

"Primrose" comes from the Middle French word primerose, meaning "first rose." Many species flower in early spring.

January 17

When wrens are seen in winter, expect snow.

January 18

*A*frican violets are stunning tropical plants. Their cheerful flowers perched just above a neat rosette of dark-green, fuzzy leaves may bloom constantly throughout the year. In addition to standard varieties, there are miniature African violets and trailing forms that can be grown in hanging pots.

January 19

B aron Walter von Saint-Paul discovered the African violet in 1892. The genus *Saintpaulia* was named after the baron. The species name, *ionantha*, from the Greek, means "having flowers like the violet's."

January 20

*T*he bright summer blossoms of coneflowers (*Echinacea spp.*) dry and darken at the end of the growing season. The seeds are a favorite of goldfinches, and the dried seed heads form a striking contrast against the winter snow.

January 21

Pink jasmine (*Jasminum polyanthum*) is hardy to Zone 8. This evergreen vine is one of the easiest jasmines to grow indoors — just give it a sunny, cool spot. In winter, pink buds appear that open to bright white, fragrant blossoms. The plant's twining nature makes it perfect for hanging baskets.

January 22

Franklinia alatamaha, also called Ben Franklin's tree, has beautiful white flowers and grows best in Zones 6 to 8.

January 23

*M*ost bromeliad varieties prefer loose, coarse potting soil with good drainage. Overwatering will cause the plant foliage to drop.

January 24

When oak trees bend with snow in January, good crops may be expected.

January 25

An espalier is sure to be an eye-catcher in your garden. These trees or shrubs, pruned so that they grow in a single plane, are ideal for small garden spaces or patios, and can be grown on wire frames and used as hedges, screens, garden dividers, or borders for paths. A single espaliered plant may be displayed as a piece of living art.

January 26

*H*ares take to the open country before a snowstorm.

January 27

C rop seeds from more than 100 countries reside in
Norway's Svalbard Global Seed Vault near the Arctic
Circle. In an effort to protect biodiversity, the facility can store
2 billion seeds.

January 28

When the weather is cold and there is no snow on the ground, set water out for the birds. Or, you may fill the birdbath with cracked ice.

January 29

_____

_J_ asmine releases its fragrance at night. The scent is exceptionally strong during a waxing moon.

January 30/31

_____

The cheerful, bright flowers of primroses can be enjoyed inside the home as well as outdoors. Certain species, such as the dainty fairy primrose (*Primula malacoides*) and the Polyantha primrose (*P. x polyantha*), do especially well as houseplants. Place them in a cool spot with indirect sunlight and keep the soil moist. The plants will reward you with spectacular color in late winter and early spring. Depending on the species, flower color may be white, red, pink, yellow, blue, or lilac.

February 1

*T*o Be a Bee

Q: What are the life stages of a honeybee?

A: The queen lays up to 3,000 eggs per day, each in a cell of the honeycomb. An egg hatches in about three days, whereupon a larva emerges. The larva goes through several stages (instars) for about six days, and then a worker bee seals it in its cell with a cap of wax. The larva then changes to a pupa, and in about 8 to 14 days emerges as an adult. Queens develop in about 16 days, workers in 21 days, and drones within 24 days.

February 2

_____
_____
_____
_____
_____
_____
_____
_____
_____
_____
_____
_____
_____
_____
_____
_____
_____
_____
_____
_____
_____
_____
_____

While creating its den, a groundhog typically removes over 700 pounds of soil.

February 3

Save containers for seed-starting, such as toilet paper rolls cut in half, plastic frozen dinner trays, or yogurt cups.

February 4

Notes

S ay It With Flowers.
February's flower, the primrose, means silent love
in the language of flowers.

February 5

*A*ccording to folklore, a witch will not enter a home if a juniper grows by the front door because she would first need to correctly count the needles.

February 6

_If_ bees get out in February, the next day will be windy and rainy.

February 7

_C_ ut forsythia branches and plunge them into hot water,
then cool water, to force them to bloom indoors.

February 8

Start cooking root vegetables in cold water; aboveground vegetables, in boiling water.

February 9

_____
_____
_____
_____
_____
_____
_____
_____
_____
_____
_____
_____
_____
_____
_____
_____
_____
_____
_____
_____
_____
_____
_____
_____
_____

Weather lore says that when it storms on the first Sunday in the month, it will storm every Sunday.

February 10

*P*rune any tree limbs that have been damaged by ice and snow.

February 11

_____
_____
_____
_____
_____
_____
_____
_____
_____
_____
_____
_____
_____
_____
_____
_____
_____
_____
_____
_____
_____
_____
_____
_____
_____
_____
_____

*W*arm-climate gardeners can set out onions, cabbage, and lettuce as soon as the crocuses bloom.

February 12

Notes

Out of dry wood? Ash wet or ash dry,
A king shall warm his slippers by.

February 13

Now is the time to clean birdhouses and put up new ones so that they will be ready when feathered friends return.

February 14

*H*ydrangeas and goldenrod attract soldier beetles, which feed on aphids and spider mites.

February 15

The blossoms of hybrid hellebores (*Helleborus x hybridus*) are welcome sights in wintertime. The flowers come in a variety of colors, patterns, and shapes. What look like petals are actually modified leaves that last for weeks. Hellebores require some shade and moisture but are easy to grow.

February 16

*T*hunder in February frightens the maple syrup back into the ground.

February 17

The avocado is a dense, fast-growing evergreen. It does well in the mild-winter areas of California, Florida, and Hawaii.

February 18

For good luck, hang garlic bulbs on the mantel.

February 19

*I*f a bee flies into the house, it is a sign of good luck. However, the luck will hold only if the bee is allowed either to stay or to fly out of the house of its own accord. It is considered unlucky to kill a bee.

February 20

Before adding daffodils to a vase of tulips, soak them in a separate container for 24 hours; do not recut.

February 21

S our cherries, such as 'Montmorency,' are perfect for pies and
jams. Plant the trees in full sun in a spot with well-drained
soil and good air circulation. For smaller spaces, consider dwarf
trees such as 'North Star.' Unlike most sweet types, sour cherries
do not need another tree for pollination. Allow about 3 to 5 years
for young trees to start fruiting. The longer you leave these tart
cherries on the tree, the sweeter they'll be.

February 22

NOTES

$\mathcal{A}$t Mount Vernon, George Washington experimented with many seed varieties, practiced crop rotation, tried dozens of fertilizers, and designed a 16-sided barn.

February 23

When thinning herbs, transplant the extras of basil, marjoram, sage, and thyme. Unlike deep-rooted herbs such as dill and parsley, these herbs will thrive in their new spots.

February 24

*V*ertical vegetable gardening saves space and enables you to reach the harvest more easily. It also increases air circulation around crops, reducing the chance of fungal diseases developing. Train climbing plants, such as cucumbers, pole beans, squashes, and tomatoes, to grow up A-frames, arbors, cages, teepees, or trellises. Or, tie them to upright strings or secure them to holdfasts along a wall or fence. Add flowering vines, such as climbing nasturtiums, for a colorful display. Water regularly.

February 25

Heavy north winds bode a fruitful year.

February 26

*B*leeding heart (*Dicentra spectabilis*) is a beautiful perennial for shade where the soil is moist but well drained. Look for 'Alba' and 'Pantaloons,' both white-flowering varieties.

February 27

Remove the mulch from snowdrops and crocuses so that the shoots can come through. Keep other spring bulbs lightly covered.

February 28/29

_H_ ellebore's common name is Lenten Rose because it
blooms around the beginning of Lent.

March 1

Keep off the grass this month if it's soggy. Too much pressure will compact the soil and inhibit the rooting of new grass.

March 2

_____
_____
_____
_____
_____
_____
_____
_____
_____
_____
_____
_____
_____
_____
_____
_____
_____
_____
_____

*I*f you plant mint directly in the garden, it will take over. Instead, sink a 5-gallon plastic pot with the bottom cut out into the ground so that the rim is 2 inches above the surface. Fill the container with soil and plant the mint in it to discourage the roots from spreading.

March 3

*T*ransplant cabbage seedlings early so that they have enough time to mature before summer's heat.

March 4

S ay It With Flowers.
March's flower, the jonquil, means desire
in the language of flowers.

March 5

*T*he smallest seeds in the world weigh about 1/35,000,000
of an ounce. They come from certain orchids and float
in the air like dust.

March 6

_____
_____
_____
_____
_____
_____
_____
_____
_____
_____
_____
_____
_____
_____
_____
_____
_____
_____
_____
_____

Heirloom tomatoes are varieties that have been around for decades. Because they are open-pollinated, their seeds will yield plants like the parents, unlike modern hybrids. Heirlooms are fun to grow for their unusual shapes and colors. Plus, they are often more flavorful than modern types.

March 7

_____
_____
_____
_____
_____
_____
_____
_____
_____
_____
_____
_____
_____
_____
_____

*T*o Be a Bee

Q: Do all honeybees sting?

A: No, only female honeybees sting. Honeybees are fairly docile, unless they or their nest is disturbed. A worker bee will die after stinging once, because the barbed stinger remains with the victim, pulling out part of the bee's abdomen. A queen has a smooth stinger that can sting repeatedly; she uses this to kill other queens in the hive.

March 8

*U*se old salt and pepper shakers for sowing tiny seeds.
Mix the seeds with sand for better spreading.

March 9

For seeds that can be started indoors, consult a seed-starting chart or seed packet to find out how many weeks before the last predicted spring frost to sow them. Also, check to find out whether the seeds need special treatment, such as presoaking, scarification (nicking the seed coat), or stratification (chilling).

March 10

The young leaves and new flowers of red clover (*Trifolium pratense*) are edible and nutritious. They can be used in salads and soups or made into a delicious tea.

March 11

Note dates of gardening tasks such as planting and pruning. Record times of emergence, bloom, and fall color.

March 12

Notes

_C_happed lips? Dab some coconut oil on your parched pucker.

March 13

Add some clover seed to your lawn. Clover is disease-resistant and fixes nitrogen from the air. The nitrogen becomes available to other plants when the clover dies.

March 14

In March much snow,
To plants and trees much woe.

March 15

For a refreshing mouthwash: Combine 2 ounces water, ¼ teaspoon baking soda, and 1 drop each of tea tree and peppermint oil.

March 16

*G*ather "spring tonic" greens now: dandelion greens, fiddleheads, and leeks.

March 17

Cabbage seeds will grow well if you sow them today while wearing your nightclothes.

March 18

Thin seedlings growing in flats by scissoring them off at soil level, so as not to disturb the roots of neighboring plants.

March 19

Notes

Welcome worms to your garden. They do wonders for the soil — improving aeration, moisture retention, and structure.

March 20

*R*obins arrive now with this advice:
"Cheer up, cheerily, cheer up!"

March 21

Shade gardens offer many options for beautiful displays of color and texture, including a variety of soothing green hues. Bleeding hearts (shown here), brunnera, columbines, hellebores, primroses, and wild blue phlox are just some of the flowers that can brighten a dark area in springtime.

March 22

_____

*T*he mild, tart, and tangy flavor of heirloom tomato 'Green Zebra' makes this variety perfect for use in homemade salsa.

March 23

When harvesting sour cherries, cut them from the tree rather than risk damage by pulling the stalks.

March 24

_____
_____
_____
_____
_____
_____
_____
_____
_____
_____
_____
_____
_____
_____
_____
_____
_____
_____
_____
_____
_____
_____
_____

Robins eat lots of earthworms in the morning.
Later in the day, they dine mostly on soft fruit.

March 25

The word "tarragon" originates from the Arabic word tarkhun, or "dragon," due to the serpentine appearance of its roots.

March 26

Listen for the spring "peepers" now!

March 27

*I*t is lucky to see the first sliver of a new moon "clear of the brush," meaning that vegetation does not block the view.

March 28

A ladybug may eat as many as 5,000 aphids during its lifetime.

March 29

_____

The last three days of March are called the borrowing days, generally thought to be cold and stormy.

March 30/31

Today, many lawn enthusiasts are adding clover. White clover crowds out broadleaf weeds while it grows harmoniously with grass. It will thrive in poorly drained and shady areas and is also extremely drought-resistant. As a legume, clover has the ability to take nitrogen from the air and convert it to fertilizer.

April 1

According to folklore, the number of puffs it takes to remove all the seeds from a dandelion is the number of years it will be before you are married.

April 2

Notes

_____
_____
_____
_____
_____
_____
_____
_____
_____
_____
_____
_____
_____
_____
_____
_____
_____
_____
_____
_____
_____
_____
_____
_____

*A*fter transplanting a rosebush, water it daily for the first week, then water every three days.

April 3

Notes

If the first three days in April be foggy,
Rain in June will make the lanes boggy.

April 4

Notes

After the last spring frost, transplant Easter lilies outdoors in full sun and rich, well-drained soil. Set bulbs 6 to 8 inches deep; add 2 inches of mulch.

April 5

The best time to apply fertilizer is before it rains.

April 6

Grasshopper eggs hatch when lilacs bloom.

April 7

Some seeds disperse from their capsule when falling raindrops trigger a springboard mechanism. Certain kalanchoes use this method.

April 8

*R*oses should not be planted if the soil is still damp and muddy.

April 9

_____
_____
_____
_____
_____
_____
_____
_____
_____
_____
_____
_____
_____
_____
_____
_____
_____
_____
_____
_____
_____
_____
_____

Say It With Flowers.
April's flower, the sweet pea, indicates delicate pleasure in the language of flowers.

April 10

Notes

April's Full Pink Moon is also known
as the Little Frogs Croak Moon.

April 11

W ait to prune camellias, forsythia, lilac, quince, and other ornamental spring-flowering shrubs until after they finish blooming.

April 12

NOTES

*L*arge-fruit crabapple varieties such as 'Dolgo' are wildlife favorites.

April 13

Notes

America's National Tree, the oak, can start to produce acorns when it is 20 years old but sometimes may wait as much as 50 years before it begins.

April 14

Notes

_____
_____
_____
_____
_____
_____
_____
_____
_____
_____
_____
_____
_____
_____
_____
_____
_____
_____
_____
_____
_____
_____
_____
_____

Grapes need full sun and can tolerate most any soil with good drainage.

April 15

NOTES

Color your Easter eggs with natural dyes. Use blueberries, purple grapes, beets, onion skins, and spinach leaves.

April 16

Notes

When the weather is warm, leave cold frames open throughout the day to harden off seedlings that are to be set out later.

April 17

_____
_____
_____
_____
_____
_____
_____
_____
_____
_____
_____
_____
_____
_____
_____
_____

To Be a Bee

Q: How many eyes does a honeybee have?

A: Five. A honeybee has two compound eyes made of thousands of hexagonal facets, or lenses, that are excellent for detecting motion. (Drones have more facets than worker and queen bees.) There are also three simple eyes, called "ocelli," that are located above the compound eyes. Ocelli can detect changes in light intensity.

April 18

*I*t may take years for a trillium to recover after its flower
or leaves have been picked. Because of this, laws in some
regions prohibit harvesting certain species.

April 19

NOTES

St. George is the patron saint of farmers and field workers.

April 20

Native lady beetles, as well as the naturalized, multicolored, Asian lady beetles, are some of the cuter beneficial insects in the garden. Both larvae and adults (also called ladybugs or ladybirds) eat aphids, mites, scale, thrips, and other small, soft-bodied insects or insect eggs. Attract them with pollen and nectar sources such as angelica, coreopsis, dill, fennel, tansy, or yarrow; they like dandelions and goldenrod, too.

April 21

NOTES

Recycle used coffee grounds by working them into the soil where you intend to plant carrots. This helps to repel root maggots and to provide nitrogen.

April 22

Notes

To keep rabbits away, put soap shavings in small drawstring bags and place them around the garden.

April 23

Notes

To condition hair, combine 2 tablespoons of honey with one mashed avocado. Apply to the scalp, wait for 20 minutes, and then rinse.

April 24

There are 75 different species of snowdrops (*Galanthus nivalis*), which bloom in early spring. They are all white!

April 25

To dream of crocuses signifies happy new beginnings.

April 26

Grapevines fruit on shoots that emerge in spring from 1-year-old canes. If quality, rather than quantity, is the focus, thin developing grapes in spring and summer. Leave one bunch per shoot. The remaining cluster will develop larger berries and a sweeter taste.

April 27

Notes

_____
_____
_____
_____
_____
_____
_____
_____
_____
_____
_____
_____
_____
_____
_____
_____
_____
_____
_____
_____
_____
_____
_____
_____

The fresh petals of clove pinks (*Dianthus caryophyllus*) can be used in mulled wines, salads, and desserts.

April 28

Notes

For a good-tempered relationship, buy an engagement ring on a Wednesday.

April 29

Notes

Because of their voracious appetite for insects, praying mantises are considered a friend to farmers and gardeners. Although they may eat other beneficial insects (and, occasionally, each other), their preference is for the sucking and cutting insects that do the greatest damage to crops.

April 30

Whether tricolored, bicolored, or solid, pansies present a cheerful display during cooler temperatures. The perky petals are edible, too. Although short-lived perennials, pansies usually are grown as annuals. You also may find new pansies popping up next growing season, because the plants tend to self-sow.

May 1

On May Day in France, it is traditional to give a sprig of
lily-of-the-valley to friends and family for luck.

May 2

Notes

_____

_____

_____

_____

_____

_____

_____

_____

_____

_____

_____

_____

_____

_____

_____

_____

_____

_____

_____

_____

_____

_____

_____

_____

'Queen Victoria' cardinal flower (*Lobelia*) features reddish-bronze foliage and striking red flowers that attract hummingbirds and butterflies.

May 3

The month of May is famous for its flowers, and shrubs contribute their fair share to the show. Among the crowd-pleasers are azaleas, deutzias, mock orange, spireas, and viburnums, which produce eye-popping color against the young green landscape. And who can resist the color and fragrance of lilacs?

May 4

_A_zaleas have long been adored for their brightly colored flowers and outstanding form and foliage. There are azaleas for just about every landscape situation: low-growing to tall or weeping; deciduous to evergreen; and spring- to summer-blooming.

May 5

To deter squash bugs from attacking pumpkin vines,
plant catnip, marigolds, mint, nasturtiums, petunias,
or radishes nearby.

May 6

_G_ive peonies plenty of water to fill out the flower buds.
For even larger blooms, pinch off any small side buds
and leave the terminal one.

May 7

To Be a Bee

Q: What do honeybees eat?

A queen is fed solely on royal jelly (a glandular secretion of a worker bee) throughout her life. Worker bees are fed exclusively on royal jelly until they are three days old. After that, their diet changes to pollen, honey, nectar, and water; the percentages change as the bees age. Drones have a diet similar to that of worker bees, although in different proportions.

May 8

Although peonies require a chilling period to set buds, early-blooming, single, or Japanese cultivars may do well in the south up to Zone 8.

May 9

_I_t is good luck to meet a chimney sweep
on the way to your wedding.

May 10

─────────────────────────────────
─────────────────────────────────
─────────────────────────────────
─────────────────────────────────
─────────────────────────────────
─────────────────────────────────
─────────────────────────────────
─────────────────────────────────
─────────────────────────────────
─────────────────────────────────
─────────────────────────────────
─────────────────────────────────
─────────────────────────────────
─────────────────────────────────
─────────────────────────────────
─────────────────────────────────
─────────────────────────────────
─────────────────────────────────
─────────────────────────────────
─────────────────────────────────
─────────────────────────────────
─────────────────────────────────

*S*ay It With Flowers.
May's flower, the hawthorn, means hope
in the language of flowers.

May 11

To attract a variety of butterflies and moths, plant an herb garden that includes dill, parsley, common rue, sage, and thyme.

May 12

G row carrots in a container filled with light, fluffy soil. The seeds are slow to germinate and could take as long as three weeks. Keep the soil moist until they're up.

May 13

W atch carefully for falling temperatures: Now is often a time when last frosts arrive in parts of the country.

May 14

Notes

*G*ive hot peppers a head start: Before planting,
soak the seeds overnight in warm water.

May 15

Notes

Corn planted under a waning moon grows slower but yields larger ears.

May 16

Notes

Brighten up your garden with native Mexican plants such as cosmos, dahlias, marigolds, and zinnias.

May 17

NOTES

_A_ homemade organic soil mix should be 20 to 50 percent
high-quality, mature compost.

May 18

Notes

Water newly transplanted seedlings with 2 gallons of warm water combined with 1 package of dry yeast.

May 19

_____
_____
_____
_____
_____
_____
_____
_____
_____
_____
_____
_____
_____
_____
_____
_____
_____
_____
_____
_____
_____

*I*f bees stay at home, rain will soon come; if they fly away, fine will be the day.

May 20

_T_oss a penny overboard to ensure a safe journey at sea.

May 21

*G*et your melons in the ground as soon as all danger of
frost is past. Plant them in well-drained soil in full sun.

May 22

Notes

Wool will grow back more fully if a sheep is sheared during the light of the moon (between the new and full phases).

May 23

Notes

A cold May is kindly and fills the barn finely.

May 24

Notes

Birthday of Robert B. Thomas, founder of *The Old Farmer's Almanac*.

May 25

When planting corn, put five grains to the hill, saying: One for the blackbird, one for the crow, one for the cutworm, and one to grow.

May 26

To attract butterflies, plant bright-color asters, coneflowers, and verbena.

May 27

_A_ watermelon seed flew 68 feet 9⅛ inches, setting a world record in 1989. The triumphant spitter was Lee Wheelis, who was a contestant at the Luling (Texas) Watermelon Thump Festival.

May 28

———————————————————————————————
———————————————————————————————
———————————————————————————————
———————————————————————————————
———————————————————————————————
———————————————————————————————
———————————————————————————————
———————————————————————————————
———————————————————————————————
———————————————————————————————
———————————————————————————————
———————————————————————————————
———————————————————————————————
———————————————————————————————
———————————————————————————————
———————————————————————————————
———————————————————————————————
———————————————————————————————
———————————————————————————————
———————————————————————————————
———————————————————————————————
———————————————————————————————
———————————————————————————————
———————————————————————————————
———————————————————————————————
———————————————————————————————

Broccoli raab, collards, horseradish, and kale are all members of the mustard family.

May 29

*H*erbs that flourish in shade include sweet cicely, comfrey, and mint.

May 30/31

Notes

Bury seaweed in garden soil: Root crops will love it.

June 1

_____

_____

_____

_____

_____

_____

_____

_____

_____

_____

_____

_____

_____

_____

_____

_____

_____

_____

_____

S trawberry jars are a fun way to grow this delectable fruit. The jars have pockets along the sides for plants as well as an opening on the top. Simply fill the jar with soil up to the first pocket and pop a plant into the hole. Repeat for the other pockets, and continue filling with soil until the level reaches 1 to 2 inches below the top. Plant two or three plants at the top, then fill the jar with soil until it's level with the rim. Set in full sun, water the top and pockets, and enjoy!

June 2

Notes

_____

Seeds normally don't appear in store-bought pineapples, which are bred to be seedless. In the wild, however, a seed may develop in each of the tiny, diamond-shape fruitlets that form the pineapple.

June 3

While you're cooking, set a glass baking dish on your cookbook to hold it open and keep it clean.

June 4

Notes

Soak rusty garden tools for several hours in a bucket of cool, strong black tea.

June 5

*H*ollyhock blooms will last longer if you thin the flower buds. Pinch off some of the buds when small.

June 6

Notes

A wet June makes a dry September.

June 7

NOTES

_____

_____

_____

_____

_____

_____

_____

_____

_____

_____

_____

_____

_____

_____

_____

_____

_____

_____

_____

_____

S t. John's wort (*Hypericum perforatum*) blooms during the Nativity of St. John the Baptist (June 24). This is also Midsummer Day, and harvesting the herb at this time was thought to give it special powers. The plant was hung over the front door as an amulet of protection from evil spirits, lightning, and fire.

June 8

The perennial yellow flag iris (*Iris pseudacorus*) can become invasive and is banned in some states.

June 9

Spiders in motion indicate rain.

June 10

NOTES

_H_ ollyhocks bring a cheerful vertical element to fresh flower arrangements. After you pick them, trim the hollow stem ends, turn them upside down, fill each with water, and then quickly place the stems in vase water. Arrange with other flowers, such as baby's-breath, bellflowers, phlox, and roses.

June 11

*T*o preserve the luck of the household, pour a small amount of milk on the doorstep today.

June 12

_____
_____
_____
_____
_____
_____
_____
_____
_____
_____
_____
_____
_____
_____
_____
_____
_____
_____
_____
_____
_____

A successful butterfly garden includes plants that provide either nectar for adult butterflies or food and shelter for their larvae. Different butterflies favor different plants. Some are pickier than others, preferring just a few plants to a smorgasbord. Be sure to do a bit of research before planting time.

June 13

_____
_____
_____
_____
_____
_____
_____
_____
_____
_____
_____
_____
_____
_____
_____
_____
_____
_____
_____
_____
_____
_____
_____

To confuse berry-eating birds, put small red objects such as bottle caps or painted rocks in between your strawberry plants when they just start to flower.

June 14

Notes

*D*o you know the difference? Azaleas are smaller, with small deciduous or evergreen leaves. Rhododendrons are usually evergreen and most have large leaves that are long, broad, and leathery. Usually, azaleas have five stamens while rhododendrons have ten.

June 15

Notes

Garnish summer salads with hollyhock flowers —
they're edible!

June 16

For centuries, gardeners have been fascinated with the beauty and aerobatics of hummingbirds. While whizzing about the garden, hummingbirds expend so much energy that they must eat almost constantly from sunrise to sunset and visit over a thousand flowers every day.

June 17

 slice of lemon will clean berry-stained fingers.

June 18

_____
_____
_____
_____
_____
_____
_____
_____
_____
_____
_____
_____
_____
_____
_____
_____
_____
_____
_____
_____
_____
_____
_____
_____
_____
_____
_____

S ay It With Flowers.
June's flower, the honeysuckle, indicates fidelity
in the language of flowers.

June 19

Notes

_____
_____
_____
_____
_____
_____
_____
_____
_____
_____
_____
_____
_____
_____
_____
_____
_____
_____
_____
_____
_____
_____
_____

*P*each trees can be thinned now. There should be about six to eight inches between the fruit.

June 20

_____
_____
_____
_____
_____
_____
_____
_____
_____
_____
_____
_____
_____
_____
_____
_____
_____
_____
_____
_____
_____
_____
_____
_____

*W*hen buying seedlings, bigger is not always better. The smaller plant may be less developed but will root faster in your garden. Look for dark-green leaves and a thick stem with no yellowing or shriveling.

June 21

*T*o Be a Bee

Q: What is a honeybee swarm?

A: A swarm is a group of bees that leaves the original colony, usually because of overcrowding. This most often occurs in late spring to early summer. The swarm will contain the old queen, a few drones, and thousands of worker bees — about half of the colony. The group leaves the hive and settles on a tree branch or other object until scouts can find a suitable nesting site, such as a tree cavity. The process takes a few hours to a day or so. Honeybee swarms are not normally aggressive unless provoked.

June 22

Notes

_____
_____
_____
_____
_____
_____
_____
_____
_____
_____
_____
_____
_____
_____
_____
_____
_____
_____
_____
_____
_____
_____
_____

_G_ive your garden an inch of water every week, watering
deeply around the roots each time.

June 23

Notes

Pinch off the tops of sweet pea plants to encourage bushy growth.

June 24

Notes

In French, alpine strawberries are called fraises des bois, meaning "strawberries of the woods."

June 25

When working in the garden, wrap a strip of flypaper around your hat and fasten it with a paper clip to catch swarming bugs.

June 26

Notes

Red currant tomatoes contain 40 times more lycopene than domestic tomatoes. This antioxidant helps to prevent heart and kidney disease.

June 27

Notes

There are nearly 500 ladybug species in North America and about 5,000 species worldwide. They come in a wide variety of colors, including red, orange, pink, yellow, gray, brown, and black.

June 28

*P*lant French and African marigolds to control lesion and
root-knot nematodes.

June 29

_____
_____
_____
_____
_____
_____
_____
_____
_____
_____
_____
_____
_____
_____
_____
_____
_____
_____
_____
_____
_____
_____

Add a few fresh mint leaves to bathwater for a fragrant and relaxing soak.

June 30

Don't work in the garden when plants are wet.
This encourages the spread of disease.

July 1

Preserve basil by chopping up fresh leaves, placing them in ice cube trays, adding water to fill the tray, and then freezing.

July 2

Notes

_____

_____

_____

_____

_____

_____

_____

_____

_____

_____

_____

_____

_____

_____

_____

_____

_____

_____

_____

_____

_____

_____

Most climbing roses are best pruned as soon as they have finished blooming.

July 3

Notes

*T*ake cuttings from geraniums and root them in moist
sand. It helps to dry the cuttings in a shady, airy place for
several hours before planting them.

July 4

NOTES

For a patriotic garden, grow blue delphiniums (*Delphinium*) among white Shasta daisies (*Leucanthemum*) and red field poppies (*Papaver rhoeas*).

July 5

The hollow stem of lovage makes a great straw for drinking vegetable juice.

July 6

_____
_____
_____
_____
_____
_____
_____
_____
_____
_____
_____
_____
_____
_____
_____
_____
_____
_____
_____
_____
_____
_____
_____

*F*or convenience at harvest time, you might want to plant peppers together with other vegetables that you'll use in favorite recipes. For example, plant carrots, garlic, hot peppers, and onions together for pickling. Or, for a salad garden, try basil, bell peppers, scallions, spinach, and tomatoes.

July 7

Notes

Make your own hummingbird food. Dissolve 1 part sugar in 4 parts boiling water. Cool and then fill your feeder.

July 8

NOTES

Say It With Flowers.
July's flower, the larkspur, indicates lightheartedness
in the language of flowers.

July 9

NOTES

_G_ ive your cabbages a twist — this will damage the roots slightly and reduce the water intake. Too much water will cause the heads to split..

July 10

*N*OTES

*U*se chamomile, fennel, or lavender soaks for tired, swollen feet.

July 11

Grass clippings make great mulch for strawberries, raspberries, and other fruits.

July 12

orked lightning at night,
The next day clear and bright.

July 13

A baffling problem for many gardeners is what to grow in hot, dry, or gravelly areas that are too inhospitable for grass and most ground cover plants. Fortunately, there are some durable plants that will thrive under these rigorous conditions, such as shrub roses, mat-forming sedums, and bearberry.

July 14

The word "kohlrabi" came from the Italian *cavolo rapa*, meaning "cabbage turnip."

July 15

NOTES

*T*o kill mosquito larvae in rain barrels, add 1 tablespoon of vegetable oil to the water. It forms a barrier on top of the water that prevents larvae from surfacing to breathe.

July 16

Are birds eating your berries? Suspend bird netting over the plant and bury the edges, if possible.

July 17

_B_efore slicing an onion for cooking, core the root section out and replant it. It will soon grow into a new plant.

July 18

Notes

When pepper plants bloom, mix 1 tablespoon of Epsom salts in a gallon of water and then spray the solution on the plants. You will get larger plants and fruit.

July 19

Notes

*A*ir bubbles in seawater over clam beds indicate rain.

July 20

*B*ees are hardworking heroes of the garden. As they collect pollen and nectar from flowers for their hive, they also pollinate the blossoms, which results in decorative berries or edible fruit and vegetables. One way to attract these insects is to plant flowering shrubs in your yard. Butterfly bush (Buddleia), crape myrtle (*Lagerstroemia indica*), deutzia (*Deutzia*), honeysuckle (*Lonicera*), and spirea (*Spiraea*) are bee favorites. Select different varieties of shrubs that will bloom in succession, so that the bees will have food over a long period. Native plants are a plus.

July 21

Allow cherries, nectarines, peaches, and plums to ripen
fully before picking.

July 22

Notes

Peas were a bedtime snack for royalty in 17th-century France.

July 23

*I*f Japanese beetles attack your roses, gently remove them
from the bushes with a small, portable vacuum.

July 24

_F_or good luck, put a coin in your home's foundation as it is
being built.

July 25

New potatoes can be dug and enjoyed three weeks after flowers appear.

July 26

H ollyhocks grow from 6 to 8 feet tall and are among our tallest flower garden plants. Hollyhock flowers make an attractive garnish and can be used as serving cups for dips.

July 27

Notes

_____
_____
_____
_____
_____
_____
_____
_____
_____
_____
_____
_____
_____
_____
_____
_____
_____
_____
_____
_____
_____

The genus name *Apocynum* means "away from dog" in Greek. This group of plants is toxic to dogs, hence its common name, dogbane.

July 28

*B*lueberries help to slow aging.

July 29

_____

_____

_____

_____

_____

_____

_____

_____

_____

_____

_____

_____

_____

_____

*T*o Be a Bee

Q: How do honeybees make honey?

A: A worker honeybee collects nectar from hundreds of flowers to fill a special stomach called a honey sac. The nectar (about 30 to 90 percent water, with the rest complex sugars) is then passed on to worker bees in the hive, which use enzymes to convert it to digestible sugars and chemicals that protect the food against microbes. Bees help the nectar's water to evaporate by working it in their mouths and by placing it in cells and fanning it with their wings. When the honey is down to about 18 percent water, it is sealed up in the cell with wax until needed.

July 30/31

Notes

_P_ lant a second crop of lettuce, radishes, and spinach to harvest in the fall.

August 1

To harvest dry beans, wait until the pods turn yellow and start to shrivel. Then pull up the entire plant and hang it in a warm, dry place until the pods rattle (in about a week). Or, keep the plant in the ground and wait until each bean dries to the rattling stage on the plant. In either case, when the dried pods are ready, pick them and shell the beans. Let them dry out a bit more in an oven on low, and freeze for at least 2 days to kill any insects. Store in a sealed container in a cool, dry area.

August 2

Adult monarch butterflies consume nectar and liquids from fruit. To attract them, plant a few fruit trees along with plenty of flowers, especially milkweed (*Asclepias*).

August 3

Say It With Flowers.
August's flower, the gladiolus, means ready-armed
in the language of flowers..

August 4

_____
_____
_____
_____
_____
_____
_____
_____
_____
_____
_____
_____
_____
_____
_____
_____
_____
_____
_____
_____
_____
_____

*B*ury a cracked clay pot next to a couple of plants in your garden. Fill the pot with water, which will slowly seep into the ground and down to the roots of the plants.

August 5

Notes

_____
_____
_____
_____
_____
_____
_____
_____
_____
_____
_____
_____
_____
_____
_____
_____
_____
_____
_____
_____
_____
_____
_____
_____
_____
_____
_____
_____

To encourage the rooting of cuttings, add a pinch of sugar to the water.

August 6

*H*ens and chicks, cyclamen, and sedum grow well in rock
gardens because they are native to mountainous regions.

August 7

Notes

_____
_____
_____
_____
_____
_____
_____
_____
_____
_____
_____
_____
_____
_____
_____
_____
_____
_____
_____
_____
_____
_____

Treat mild sunburn with vinegar or cold peppermint tea.

August 8

Winter squash is ready to pick when the stem begins to shrivel.

August 9

---

*B*lueberries are a welcome summer treat, but the plants are fussy about soil acidity, requiring a pH between 4.0 and 5.0. Consequently, it is often easier to grow blueberries in containers. Choose dwarf cultivars, such as 'Chippewa,' 'Northblue,' 'Northsky,' 'Polaris,' or 'Tophat.' 'Sunshine Blue' is great for southern gardens. To ensure good pollination, grow two or more varieties next to each other. Provide moist, but not waterlogged, acidic soil with good drainage, and set the pots in full sun. In northern climates, provide winter protection.

August 10

_____
_____
_____
_____
_____
_____
_____
_____
_____
_____
_____
_____
_____
_____
_____
_____
_____
_____
_____
_____
_____
_____
_____
_____
_____
_____
_____

*P*ick small cucumbers for pickling about five days after the blossoms open.

August 11

For longer-lasting blooms, pick flowers in the early morning or late afternoon.

August 12

Notes

If cabbage heads begin to crack, bend them over to break the root on one side. This will help keep growth in check.

August 13

The tufts of waxy floss on milkweed seeds enable them to be blown through the air.

August 14

_____
_____
_____
_____
_____
_____
_____
_____
_____
_____
_____
_____
_____
_____
_____
_____
_____
_____

Whether planted along a fence or massed in a sunny border, the smiling faces of sunflowers are sure to brighten up even the gloomiest of days. Some varieties provide small black seeds that attract many songbirds. The bigger, striped seeds are great for snacking and attract larger birds such as jays and mourning doves.

August 15

Notes

Rule of Thumb:
Tail up? It's a goat. Tail down? It's a sheep.

August 16

If planted in the garden, basil is said to improve the flavor and vigor of tomatoes and to deter insects such as whiteflies. Use it as a mosquito repellent by crushing a few leaves and rubbing them onto your skin. In the kitchen, basil increases in flavor when cooked, so it's best to add it at the end of cooking.

August 17

_A_ cucumber can be up to 20 degrees Fahrenheit cooler on the inside than on the outside.

August 18

To Be a Bee

Q: How fast can honeybees fly?

A: A honeybee can fly up to about 15 miles per hour when searching for food. When it is returning to the hive and is laden with nectar, its speed is only about 12 miles per hour. It beats its four wings at a constant rate of about 240 beats per second and uses small strokes in arcs of about 90 degrees; each wing flips over on the return stroke. For carrying loads, the bee adjusts the arc of its wing stroke but keeps the same rate of wing beat.

August 19

_____
_____
_____
_____
_____
_____
_____
_____
_____
_____
_____
_____
_____
_____
_____
_____
_____
_____
_____
_____
_____
_____
_____

*H*arvest sweet corn when silks are dark brown, husks are green, and ears are fully developed.

August 20

Roll up your garden hose after every use and store it away from direct sunlight.

August 21

*P*ears should be picked a week or more before they become
soft on the tree. Store in a cool, dark place to ripen.

August 22

Eat tomatoes to boost your skin's natural defenses against damaging ultraviolet rays.

August 23

*S*hell beans have finished drying when your teeth can barely make a dent in a seed while biting down on it.

August 24

Notes

_____
_____
_____
_____
_____
_____
_____
_____
_____
_____
_____
_____
_____
_____
_____
_____
_____
_____

Rock gardens offer plenty of opportunities to add living color and texture. Creeping plants such as ajuga, Scotch moss, or dead nettle will wind and drape their way through the stony landscape. Plants such as wild columbine and 'Ghost' ferns, tucked into niches, serve as colorful accents.

August 25

To repel ants in your house, wipe down countertops with equal parts vinegar and water.

August 26

_____

Cacti will grow rapidly from March to September. Watering requirements vary according to plant, season, soil, humidity, and temperature. However, in general, let the soil of potted cacti dry slightly between waterings. In winter, while the plants are dormant, they should be allowed to get very dry between waterings.

August 27

*I*f the bee's in the flower,
There won't be a shower.

August 28

The magenta fruit of prickly pear cactus (called "tuna") can be used in jams, syrups, drinks, and candy. You can also eat the pads (nopales). When handling, wear gloves and goggles and use tongs. Wash and peel the fruit or pads to remove the spines and glochids (tiny prickles that can become airborne).

August 29

_____
_____
_____
_____
_____
_____
_____
_____
_____
_____
_____
_____
_____
_____
_____
_____
_____
_____
_____
_____
_____
_____

Water your garden to a depth of 3 to 5 inches. This encourages deep, healthy roots and allows longer periods between watering.

August 30/31

Fish powders or liquid fish emulsion make a fast-acting,
water-soluble fertilizer for your plants.

September 1

2 Bearded Iris in each long
herb tub. spring to early Summer

Baby, curd house gourds

This is a good time to transplant some parsley and chives
from the garden to pots for indoor use.

September 2

Mum - in hanging pot

To Be a Bee

Q: How is beeswax made?

A: A young worker honeybee eats lots of honey or nectar and later emits a drop of wax via one of eight glands on its underside. The wax hardens into a flake, which the bee (or its neighbors) then puts in its mandibles to chew and mix with secretions until it's workable. The beeswax is then used to build or repair honeycomb. About six to ten pounds of honey are needed for a colony to produce a pound of wax.

September 3

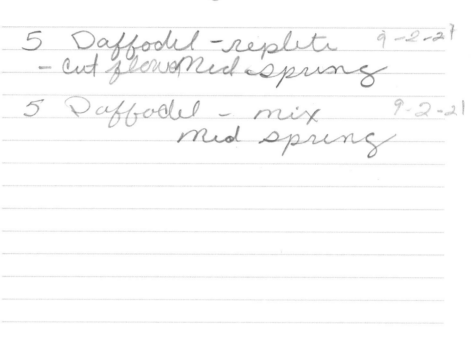

5 Daffodil - replete   9-2-2?
- cut flowers mid spring

5 Daffodil - mix   9-2-21
mid spring

Succulents are perfect for container gardens, as they can sit in the sun all day and not get thirsty. Just water thoroughly every 7 to 10 days during the growing season, depending on the plant. Succulents offer many textures, shapes, and colors for striking displays. Place them on steps, bunch them together on a patio, or line them up along a walkway. Larger specimens, such as aloes or yuccas, do well as accents. In Zone 7 and colder climes, bring succulents indoors for the winter.

September 4

*T*hunder in September indicates a good crop of grain and fruit for next year.

September 5

Apple seeds usually produce offspring that are different from the parent tree. Some may yield apples good for eating, while others may be better for cider.

September 6

*R*anging from drought-tolerant groundcovers to taller varieties, sedums are perfect for borders, beds, or containers. On sunny autumn days, bees and butterflies feed on the nectar-rich, star-shape flowers.

September 7

The Persian parrotia (*Parrotia persica*) is an attractive ornamental tree that features a haze of small, crimson, spring flowers; brilliant autumn foliage in bright-yellow, orange, and scarlet; and exfoliating bark that reveals shades of creamy-white, green, gray, and brown tones.

September 8

Notes

Pot up marigolds for continued bloom in a sunny window indoors.

September 9

_____

This is the best time of the year to reseed bare spots in old lawns.

September 10

NOTES

_____

_____

_____

_____

_____

_____

_____

_____

_____

_____

_____

_____

_____

_____

_____

_____

_____

_____

_____

_____

_____

_____

_____

_____

_____

When zucchini are plentiful, shred 1- or 2-cup portions and freeze to use in soups, stews, and nut breads in the dark of winter.

September 11

Collect and save seeds from the very best plants in your garden.

September 12

Notes

_____
_____
_____
_____
_____
_____
_____
_____
_____
_____
_____
_____
_____
_____
_____
_____
_____
_____
_____
_____
_____
_____
_____

Sweet corn requires frequent watering to produce full, healthy ears. Once the tassels appear, the plants should get one inch of water per week.

September 13

Notes

_____

S ay It With Flowers.
September's flower, the morning glory, means affection
in the language of flowers.

September 14

*D*ivide and plant peonies this month so that they will be well established before the cold weather arrives.

September 15

Onions are ready to harvest when the tops begin to weaken and fall over. Pull the plants out of the soil and let them dry in the garden for one to two days before curing and storing.

September 16

*G*ather bittersweet, strawflowers, and evergreens now for fall wreaths.

September 17

Notes

Add a teaspoon of honey to tomato-based soups to counteract acidity and improve flavor.

September 18

According to Greek tradition, a cactus placed by the front door will guard a home against evil.

September 19

Notes

_____

_____

_____

_____

_____

_____

_____

_____

_____

_____

_____

_____

_____

_____

_____

_____

_____

_____

_____

_____

_____

_____

_____

Before planting in a container, cut up an overripe banana and put it in the bottom of the pot. It will break down fast and provide beneficial organic matter for the plant.

September 20

_____
_____
_____
_____
_____
_____
_____
_____
_____
_____
_____
_____
_____
_____
_____
_____
_____
_____
_____
_____
_____
_____
_____
_____
_____
_____
_____
_____

_U_se tomato cages to support peppers.

September 21

Notes

To slow decay, leave an inch or two of stem on pumpkins and winter squash when harvesting them.

September 22

Q: What do beekeepers need when they study?
A: Some bees and quiet.

September 23

*I*f you pick a peck of peppers, you'll have a lot for pickling and canning. Choose fresh, firm, unblemished peppers with thick, waxy skins and glossy color. Cubanelle, Hungarian, jalapeño, pimiento, sweet banana, and sweet bell peppers work well. Because peppers are low in acid, you'll need to process them in a pressure canner. The exception is for pickling recipes that include an acid, such as vinegar. In that case, if the recipe is properly prepared, a boiling-water bath may be used instead. Always follow the exact amounts specified in a recipe, as the proportions are critical for safe processing.

September 24

Notes

Wood cut during the new moon is hard to split.

September 25

If you find a red-tailed bumblebee in your home,
expect a visit from a male stranger.

September 26

Notes

---

*I*f lunar gardening, harvest when the moon is between full and new and in a dry sign (Aries, Gemini, Leo, Sagittarius, or Aquarius).

September 27

The average person eats about 19 pounds of apples each year.

September 28

_____
_____
_____
_____
_____
_____
_____
_____
_____
_____
_____
_____
_____
_____
_____
_____
_____
_____
_____
_____
_____
_____
_____
_____
_____

*E*ven though spiders have as many as eight eyes, most don't see well.

September 29

Notes

_ive Moon phases in one month foretell a cold winter and a cool summer.

September 30

*I*n medieval England, as soon as the grain was harvested,
geese were allowed into the fields to feed on the
gleanings. Called green or Michaelmas geese, these birds
were traditionally served at feasts on St. Michael's day.

October 1

The banded woolly bear (or woolly worm) is the larva of the Isabella tiger moth, which is found throughout most of North America. The caterpillar has a band of reddish orange in the middle of its bristly black body. Folklore says that the greater the amount of black on a woolly bear, the greater the severity of the coming winter.

October 2

_____
_____
_____
_____
_____
_____
_____
_____
_____
_____
_____
_____
_____
_____
_____
_____
_____
_____
_____
_____
_____
_____
_____
_____
_____

Carrots can be left in the ground during a few light frosts; the cold will sweeten them. Dig them up before the ground freezes or mulch heavily to extend the harvest.

October 3

G ive evergreens, rhododendrons, and newly planted perennials a good soaking with water. Do not water newly planted bulbs.

October 4

 ow is an excellent time to give the compost pile a good turning over.

October 5

*P*eanuts are not nuts but instead are actually seeds from a leguminous plant related to peas and beans. The plant is unique because its flowers grow above ground yet the pods containing the seeds develop in the soil. Although considered a southern crop, peanuts have been grown as far north as southern Canada.

October 6

*T*o overwinter hardy mums, cut off spent flowers, but don't cut the plants back. In colder regions, provide mulch and then prune again in early spring.

October 7

*T*o Be a Bee

Q: Can honeybees see colors?

A: Honeybees can sense colors ranging from yellow and green to blue and ultraviolet. They can also detect an ultraviolet-yellow combination named "bee purple." The bees can't see red — it would appear black to them.

October 8

For every fog in October, a snow in the winter.

October 9

When seeds of the tumbleweed are ripe, the plant breaks off at the roots. Its thousands of seeds scatter across a wide area as the tumbleweed rolls along in the wind.

October 10

*N*OTES

*T*o make cut flowers last longer: Combine one part lemon-lime soda (not diet) to three parts water. Add ¼ teaspoon bleach to each quart of this solution.

October 11

Notes

The more red berries on bushes, the more frost and snow in winter.

October 12

_____
_____
_____
_____
_____
_____
_____
_____
_____
_____
_____
_____
_____
_____
_____
_____
_____
_____
_____
_____
_____
_____
_____
_____

*H*arvest Chinese cabbage when the heads are compact and firm and before flower stalks develop.

October 13

NOTES

October breezy, November wheezy, December freezy.

October 14

_____
_____
_____
_____
_____
_____
_____
_____
_____
_____
_____
_____
_____
_____
_____
_____
_____
_____
_____
_____
_____
_____

*I*n the South, spinach and onion sets may still be planted. This is also a good time to sow perennial herb seed. Try chives, fennel, sage, and thyme.

October 15

_____
_____
_____
_____
_____
_____
_____
_____
_____
_____
_____
_____
_____
_____
_____
_____
_____
_____
_____
_____
_____
_____
_____
_____
_____
_____

*W*ash outdoor planters with soapy water and a splash of bleach before storing for winter.

October 16

*A*sters are always a welcome sight with their perky white, red, pink, purple, and blue daisylike flowers. New World asters have been reclassified and now flaunt such genus names as *Symphyotrichum* (including New England and smooth asters) and *Eurybia* (including bigleaf and white wood asters).

October 17

Notes

---

*S*ay It With Flowers.
October's flower, the calendula, means joy
in the language of flowers.

October 18

Save seeds from heirloom plants to grow next year.

October 19

_____
_____
_____
_____
_____
_____
_____
_____
_____
_____
_____
_____
_____
_____
_____
_____
_____
_____
_____
_____
_____

*U*sing low-maintenance techniques can reduce much of your yard work. Large areas of ground covers or wildflowers are less labor-intensive than traditional lawns. A thick layer of organic mulch around plants will help to control weeds, conserve soil moisture, and add nutrients to the soil.

October 20

umpkins stored properly at 50° to 55°F can last up to 2 months. Keep them away from apples or other fruit.

October 21

*T*o preserve autumn leaves, dip them in melted beeswax.

October 22

_____

_____

_____

_____

_____

_____

_____

_____

_____

_____

_____

_____

_____

_____

_____

_____

_____

_____

_____

_____

_____

_____

Make not a fence more expensive or more important than the thing that is fenced.

October 23

_____
_____
_____
_____
_____
_____
_____
_____
_____
_____
_____
_____
_____
_____
_____
_____
_____

Japanese maples make perfect focal points in the landscape. Their eye-catching, palmlike leaves can be broad to feathery and are available in many combinations of green, red, pink, orange, and white. *Acer palmatum* 'Chisio' is a slow-growing tree that reaches 8 feet tall; its attractive, reddish-pink spring leaves turn green in summer and then orange-red in fall. *A. shirasawanum* 'Autumn Moon' is a 10-foot-tall tree that features scarlet spring foliage that changes to a chartreuse green tinged with rusty orange, especially in full sun; in fall, the leaves turn a striking pinkish orange.

353

October 24

*I*n Colonial times, dye made from beets was used to make pink pancakes and cake icing.

October 25

When the corn wears a coat, so must you.

October 26

Notes

*B*rush your root crops clean of any soil and store in a cool, dark place. Clipping the tops of parsnips, carrots, beets, and turnips will keep them fresher longer.

October 27

Plant scented tulips for spring. Try 'Apricot Beauty,'
'Bellona,' 'Holland's Glory,' and 'Prince of Austria.'

October 28

_____
_____
_____
_____
_____
_____
_____
_____
_____
_____
_____
_____
_____
_____
_____
_____
_____
_____

*T*rees aren't the only plants that get oohs and ahhs during the fall foliage season. Many shrubs offer spectacular displays as well. Fothergilla, a member of the witch hazel family, offers brilliant fall foliage in red, burgundy, orange, or yellow. 'Maradco' beauty bush (*Kolkwitzia amabilis* 'Maradco,' also found under the trademarked name 'Dream Catcher,' dresses in greenish yellow leaves during the growing season but switches to blazing golden-orange in fall.

October 29

_____
_____
_____
_____
_____
_____
_____
_____
_____
_____
_____
_____
_____
_____
_____
_____
_____
_____
_____
_____
_____

*M*omiji is a Japanese word for maple. It may translate as "Little baby extends its hands which are like the leaves of maple."

October 30/31

Roasted Pumpkin Seeds —
Spread 2 cups cleaned seeds in a shallow baking pan
and drizzle with 2 teaspoons oil, stirring to coat. Bake at 325°F.
Stir frequently, until seeds are golden and crunchy, about 1
hour. Serve as is or sprinkle with salt.

November 1

*P*ut your Halloween pumpkins out in the woods or fields
for wildlife to snack on.

November 2

NOTES

_____
_____
_____
_____
_____
_____
_____
_____
_____
_____
_____
_____
_____
_____
_____
_____
_____
_____
_____
_____

Many ornamental grasses have interesting stalks and seed heads that can be enjoyed during the winter months. Put off pruning the dried grass until spring, just before new growth appears.

November 3

*T*his is the time to gather cones, pods, and dried material for holiday wreaths.

November 4

_I_ f there's ice in November that will bear a duck,
there'll be nothing after but sludge and muck.

November 5

*I*t is never too late to apply lime to your lawn. The minerals in lime retain their value until the grass is ready to grow again.

November 6

NOTES

_____
_____
_____
_____
_____
_____
_____
_____
_____
_____
_____
_____
_____
_____
_____
_____
_____
_____

*W*inter squashes generally take longer to ripen than summer types, since they are harvested when the seeds are mature and the skin has toughened. You can find some unusual ones to grow in addition to the old standbys found at the grocery store, such as butternut (bottom). 'Sweet Dumpling' (middle) is a small, sweet-tasting squash that is especially good for baking. 'Sweet Meat' (top) is a favorite in the Northwest, with sweet, dry, orange flesh that does splendidly in pies.

November 7

_____
_____
_____
_____
_____
_____
_____
_____
_____
_____
_____
_____
_____
_____
_____
_____
_____
_____
_____
_____
_____
_____
_____
_____

Apply mulch to the perennial border, rose garden, and bulb plantings as soon as the ground is frozen.

November 8

*G*ive birds a high-energy snack: Cut leftover baked or roasted potatoes into bite-size chunks and place them outside.

November 9

*T*o Be a Bee
  Q: Do honeybees sleep?

A: Honeybees sometimes do exhibit sleep behavior, although not exactly as humans experience it. Research has shown, however, that their muscles relax, body temperature decreases, movement is at a minimum, and reaction to stimuli is slowed.

November 10

Notes

Seeds collected in the fall should be dried and put into envelopes before being stored in a cool, dry place.

November 11

_____
_____
_____
_____
_____
_____
_____
_____
_____
_____
_____
_____
_____
_____
_____
_____
_____
_____
_____
_____
_____
_____
_____

Ornamental corn is ideal for autumn decorations. Choose from red, rust, orange, yellow, white, blue, and multicolor. Tiny to full-size corncobs provide lots of options for arrangements. Plus, the reddish stalks of 'Ruby Queen' sweet corn make excellent cornstalk bundles.

November 12

To discourage rodents from nibbling fruit trees in winter, remove fallen leaves and fruit near the trunks.

November 13

NOTES

If you burn hardwood in your fireplace, save the ashes to use for fertilizer in the spring. Wood ashes spread around berries and fruit trees sweeten the fruit.

November 14

Notes

_____

_____

_____

_____

_____

_____

_____

_____

_____

_____

_____

_____

_____

_____

_____

_____

_____

_____

_____

_____

_____

*K*eep in mind that some ornamental grasses stay put while others like to run wild or self-sow prolifically. Place spreaders in areas where they'll have room to expand or confine them to pots as accents. Small clumpers go nicely in tiny spaces or along walkways, and larger ones serve well in beds or borders.

November 15

Cover strawberries 2 inches deep with hay or straw.

November 16

*S*tore bulbs such as dahlias, gladiolus, and caladiums in a paper bag or box filled with sawdust.

November 17

Notes

Combine one part cornmeal with four to six parts peanut butter and roll pinecones in the finished mixture. Hang them outside for the birds to snack on.

November 18

When frost threatens in warm zones, string up holiday tree lights (not the LED kind) around cold-sensitive trees to prevent damage. Keep the lights lit all night.

November 19

NOTES

*I*f your soil is dry, water shrubs and bulb beds before the ground freezes.

November 20

_A_ milkweed seed floats in air and on water because it
is attached to filaments called floss. In fact, the seed's
floss is so buoyant that it was used to insulate U.S. military life
jackets during World War II.

November 21

The Hubbard squash may have been named after
Mrs. Elizabeth Hubbard of Marblehead, Massachusetts,
in the early 1840s.

November 22

---

*F*or a healthy lawn, keep mowing the grass as long as it keeps growing.

November 23

Make a wreath to attract birds: Gather herbs, grasses, and dried seed heads of medium-size flowers with lots of seeds, such as coneflowers, daylilies, poppies, and sunflowers. Choose a straw or vine wreath base or make your own using grapevines or weeping willow branches. Use floral wire to attach the seed heads to the wreath base. Fill in with the herbs and grasses, such as northern sea oats (*Chasmanthium latifolium*) and red fountain grass (*Pennisetum setaceum* 'Rubrum'). Hang in a bird-friendly location.

November 24

A mature turkey has about 3,500 feathers.

November 25

NOTES

D rain and bring in garden hoses before the nights get too cold.

November 26

Squirrels gathering nuts in a flurry,
Will cause snow to gather in a hurry.

November 27

Notes

_____

_____

_____

_____

_____

_____

_____

_____

_____

_____

_____

_____

_____

_____

_____

_____

_____

_____

_____

_____

_____

_____

_____

*I*f the moon shows a silver shield, be not afraid to reap your fields.

November 28

The wind from northeast, neither good for man nor beast.

November 29

Notes

_A_ red bell pepper is actually just a green bell pepper that was left to mature on its stalk.

November 30

A hard frost will sweeten carrots.

December 1

If December be changeable and mild,
The whole winter will remain a child.

December 2

Notes

_____

To make a shelter for birds, heap branches from trees and shrubs loosely into a pile.

December 3

Eastern white pine (Pinus strobus) is a native Northeastern evergreen.
You will recognize it by its blue-green needles in clusters of five.

December 4

_U_se the clippings from pruned evergreens to make wreaths
and garlands.

December 5

A Saint Bernard can make its way through snow as deep as 15 feet.

December 6

*H*erald the holidays with the trumpet-shape flowers of amaryllis and paper-whites. Amaryllis bulbs form spectacularly large, flamboyant blossoms in white, red, pink, orange, or stripes perched on top of tall, bold stalks. Pungently fragrant paper-whites resemble small, delicate daffodils in white or yellow, with white to orange centers. You can buy either flower in kits, which contain bulbs, a growing medium, and a pot, or you can buy bulbs and containers separately, for more variety.

December 7

_A_ "barber" is a cold wind that brings wet snow, sleet, or spray that freezes on surfaces — including beards and hair.

December 8

Dress up gift jars of homemade jam and other canned goods by covering the lid with a piece of pretty calico cinched with a bright ribbon.

December 9

_____
_____
_____
_____
_____
_____
_____
_____
_____
_____
_____
_____
_____
_____
_____
_____
_____
_____
_____
_____
_____
_____
_____
_____
_____

*I*f you want your geraniums to bloom in the winter, put them in a sunny window and keep the temperature warm (70° to 75°F) during the day.

December 10

Notes

To make a fragrant holiday wreath, incorporate bay leaves, bittersweet, cinnamon sticks, and fresh rosemary into foot-long evergreen branches.

December 11

---

*P*otted evergreens make terrific decorations for the winter holidays and look wonderful draped with other natural materials. Be sure to choose a tree or shrub that would be appropriate for your space and climate, because after the celebrations are over, the plant will be a great addition to your yard.

December 12

For better blooms, keep cyclamen evenly moist in a cool north or east window.

December 13

*I*n cold weather, reindeer can restrict blood flow in their legs to conserve body heat.

December 14

*T*o grow an olive tree indoors, provide good drainage and place in a sunny, south-facing window.

December 15

If stored onions start to sprout, pot them up and enjoy the tasty greens all winter.

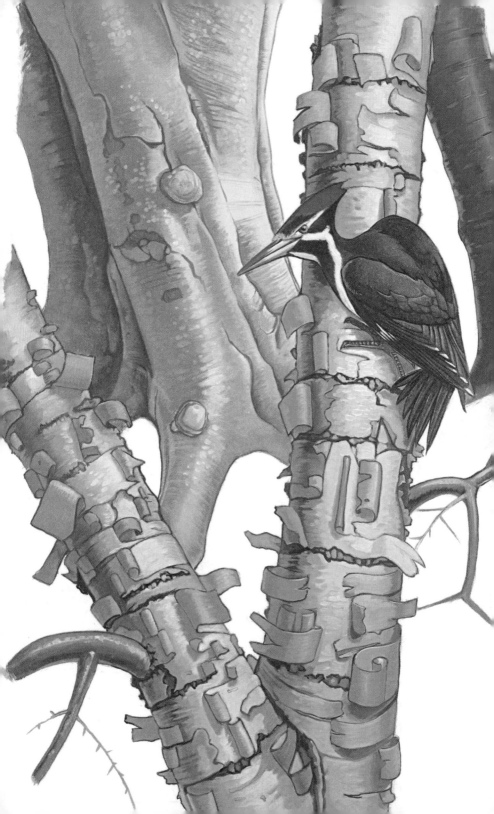

December 16

*T*rees with unusual bark add winter interest. River birch features attractive peeling bark. The American beech grows wonderful, smooth, gray bark that looks like elephant skin. Tibetan cherry has beautiful, satiny bark that shimmers in sunlight.

December 17

_____
_____
_____
_____
_____
_____
_____
_____
_____
_____
_____
_____
_____
_____
_____
_____
_____
_____
_____
_____

To Be a Bee

Q: How long do honeybees live?

A: Drones live from three to ten weeks; if food is scarce or winter arrives, they are usually evicted from the hive. A worker bee lasts about four weeks to six months, depending on the time of year; a bee in summer will live a shorter life. The queen can live from two to five years.

December 18

*P*ut out plenty of high-calorie birdseed and suet for the birds now.

December 19

Spend these winter evenings reading seed catalogs and planning your next garden. Make your list but don't mail it right away; a pause now will give you a chance to change your mind tomorrow.

December 20

*T*o protect perennials from freezing and thawing, shovel snow over them; in areas with little snowfall, add 2 to 3 inches of mulch.

December 21

Celebrate! The days are starting to get longer.

December 22

Notes

_____
_____
_____
_____
_____
_____
_____
_____
_____
_____
_____
_____
_____
_____
_____
_____
_____
_____
_____
_____
_____
_____
_____
_____
_____

 dream of grinding coffee suggests domestic happiness.

December 23

*T*he Colorado blue spruce (*Picea pungens*) is more drought
tolerant than other spruces, but it prefers moist, rich soil
and full sunlight.

December 24

_____
_____
_____
_____
_____
_____
_____
_____
_____
_____
_____
_____
_____
_____
_____
_____
_____
_____
_____
_____
_____
_____
_____
_____
_____
_____
_____
_____

The Yule log, lit on Christmas Eve, symbolizes an end to old feuds and grudges.

December 25

NOTES

On this day in 1906, "O Holy Night" was played on the world's first radio broadcast.

December 26

S ay It With Flowers.
December's flower, the holly, means foresight
in the language of flowers.

December 27

A group of goldfinches is called a charm; rhinoceroses, a crash; trout, a hover.

Notes

Notes

NOTES

NOTES